HAIKU
EVOLUTION

by

LEON TEFFT

Haiku Evolution

Copyright © 2025 by Leon Tefft

Published by Upcountry Press LLC

All rights reserved.

This is a work of fiction. Names, characters, places and incidents either are the products of the author's imagination or are used fictitiously. Any resemblance to actual persons, living or dead, businesses, companies, events or locales is entirely coincidental.

FIRST EDITION

ISBN: 979-8-9910818-2-5

Written and edited by Leon Tefft

LEONTEFFT.COM

CONTENTS

To Dorian Trahan

*For always encouraging me to find my voice and
allowing me the freedom to follow it.*

*From that early creative spark through now and always,
this book is dedicated to your free spirit.*

Introduction

This book you hold in your hands—*Haiku Evolution*—is my second published work and a direct follow-up to *Haiku Traditions*. Much effort has gone into its content and design to ensure entertainment and value for you, the reader. I'm sincerely grateful for your interest in my poetry.

Haiku Traditions and *Haiku Evolution* can be read independently; however, they were created to complement one another, with each book offering something unique for all readers to learn from and enjoy.

Haiku Evolution reflects my writing journey, transitioning from the traditional 5-7-5 syllable pattern haiku to a modern, free-form style. This change, where elegance and simplicity take precedence over syllables, has been a significant part of my poetry's evolution. Typically, I now write only in the free-form style presented in this book.

But it was not always this way for me. I adhered to the 5-7-5 tradition for decades, following common guidelines to create picturesque portraits of haiku. It's what I was taught and all I knew. During that time, on occasions when I would read free-form haiku, I often thought little of it. The writing style seemed silly and usually made no sense whatsoever. It seemed like lazy writing to me and creatively misguided. I often asked myself, "What does one part of this haiku have to do with the rest of it? Are these short, odd poems even really haiku?"

If you're of that same mindset, *Haiku Evolution* is the ideal book for you. Its aim is to introduce readers and writers of traditional haiku to a style beyond the 5-7-5 tradition in a meaningful way that makes sense. That's not to project free-form as a better haiku style, but rather a different style. I have great respect for the 5-7-5 tradition and understand its unique beauty. Although I prefer to read and write free-form haiku for many reasons, this preference doesn't prompt me to think less of practitioners of the 5-7-5 tradition as many critics of the form choose to do. I'm an advocate of poets writing whatever they enjoy writing and letting the critics be damned.

Like *Haiku Traditions*, this book is designed to be accessible to a broad audience. It features 300 original poems, including 220 haiku, 40 senryu, 30 tanka and 10 haibun. Each section is introduced in a way that invites all readers to understand what they're reading and engage with the poetry, regardless of their familiarity with the forms.

Initially, I had a different title in mind for this book. As I was writing the material for it over many months, I was also deep into studying haiku and other short-form poetry. As I adapted to new learning, it became clear that my writing style began to change. My skills advanced, and my poetry evolved as I produced the content for this book. Each chapter in this book starts with earlier writing, leading to the most recent poems toward the end. As I reviewed each chapter, the evolution in style was evident to me and might be to you as well. Poems gradually transform from a traditional sense to a more elegant style emphasizing conciseness.

This progression of growth and change adds another dimension to the title, *Haiku Evolution*. Supposing I write more books after this one, I expect to find the same pattern happening again as long as I'm experiencing growth and improvement. I'll just have to come up with appropriate book titles!

Each of these 300 poems offers a unique opportunity for contemplation, inviting you to embark on a journey of personal introspection. The interpretations you draw from them are uniquely yours to discover, guided by your own experiences and feelings as you immerse yourself in the imagery and emotional flow of the words. I encourage you to pause and reflect after each poem, allowing them to resonate within you. I hope you encounter surprising insights and uncover meaning that enhances your understanding of poetry and yourself.

I'd love to hear your thoughts and interpretations of the poems in this book. Poetry is a dialogue between the poet and the reader. Feel free to connect with me on my author website at LEONTEFFT.COM.

SECTION I
HAIKU

What is Haiku?

Haiku, at its core, is a simple yet profound form of poetry that anyone can readily try their hand at. My introduction to haiku came during high school in a creative writing class. My teacher taught me the same information that most people likely become familiar with when they first discover haiku, which distills into two basic rules:

1. haiku comprises three lines that do not need to rhyme
2. haiku adheres to a 5-7-5 syllable count pattern

Armed with this knowledge, anyone who can string together a series of words in three lines following the sacred syllable pattern can consider themselves a poet. Let's experiment.

the sky is deep blue
puffy white clouds float along
on a sunny day

Let's see: three lines, five syllables in the first line, seven in the second, five again in the third. Bingo! I'm a haiku poet!

Not exactly. I've written what amounts to little more than a journal entry or a weather report. It is merely an observation, not a haiku. It may just need some spicing up. Let's try again.

the sky is azure
alabaster clouds drift by
on a sunlit day

Now we're talking, right?

Again, not exactly.

Replacing some of the words with more sophisticated and less common ones may sound poetic, but the message is still the same journal entry or weather report. Let's try one more time.

azure sky
among clouds
thoughts drift

You've probably noticed I broke a cardinal rule and disregarded the 5-7-5 syllable pattern for one that adds up to 3-3-2. And what does "thinking" have to do with the sky? This poem goes against common knowledge of what haiku should be, yet a haiku emerges in this final form. Allow me to explain how we arrived here.

Casting Aside the Rule of Syllables

Haiku, a poetic form that traces its origins to 13th-century Japan, was initially used as the opening phrase in long-form renga poetry. During Japan's Edo Period in the 16th century, renowned masters of the form, including Matsuo Basho (1644-1694), Yosa Buson (1716-1784) and Kobayashi Issa (1763-1828), practiced the standalone haiku, initially known as *hokku*. By the 19th century, hokku had evolved into the current form known as haiku. While traditional haiku poets focused on nature and seasonal elements, contemporary haiku poets can freely explore any subject.

The 5-7-5 syllable pattern, or 17-syllable count, is based on the Japanese "*on*," which refers to phonetic units arranged in a haiku but are not identical to syllables. When translated to another language from Japanese, the *on* of a haiku typically will not match the new language form in syllables—likewise, writing a 17-syllable haiku in English, for example, and translating it to Japanese results in a version that will probably have many more *on* than desired.

Because syllable counts can often differ significantly during translation from one language to another, writers can opt for a free-form style and disregard the traditional haiku rule of 17 syllables in a 5-7-5 pattern. Furthermore, there are other reasons to abandon this rule.

Less is More

A persuasive characteristic of haiku is its ability to evoke strong impressions with just a few carefully chosen words. A well-crafted haiku captures a fleeting moment in the present tense and delivers it with clarity and conciseness. Reading a haiku should feel like a seamless stream of consciousness, conveying a sense of "being there" in the moment.

The completed haiku I previously wrote comprises just six words using eight syllables. It succeeds at being direct and concise in portraying a complete picture. To add unnecessary or repetitive words to a haiku to fulfill a 17-syllable count rule adds excess bulk and can spoil the elegance of the haiku.

Kigo: Seasons Summarized in a Word

Kigo, or seasonal word, is a natural element that lends itself well to writing haiku. The use of kigo provides a setting for seasonal haiku, often with just a single word, without having to describe a scene or image in greater detail, thereby adding to the "less is more" characteristic of composing clear and concise haiku.

Here are some common examples of seasonal kigo words:

Spring: sakura or cherry blossoms, wisteria, hazy moon, fawn, frog, robin, birdsong, breeze, kite

Summer: lotus, rose, strawberry, beach, meadow, butterfly, dragonfly, cicada, mosquito, ice cream

Autumn: chrysanthemum, maple, apple, fog, frost, deer, cricket, crow, pumpkin, harvest, scarecrow

Winter: crocus, poinsettia, holly, snow, ice, cold moon, crane, swan, wolf, oyster, bonfire, caroling

Some of these are obvious, such as "strawberry" or "snow." Strawberries grow in summer, and snow falls in winter. Others cross blurred lines between seasons. You can fly a kite on any windy day of the year or see a maple tree during any season. Butterflies are common during spring, summer and autumn. "Rain" is considered a summer season kigo, but it doesn't only rain during summer.

Kigo blurs lines elsewhere, too. Seasonal words can mean different things to people depending on where they live or their culture. "Snow" means more than just winter to someone living in Alaska and something less to people of Egypt or Fiji. Ice cream reminds me of hot summer days, but what does it mean to someone who doesn't eat ice cream?

When writing seasonal haiku, I regard kigo as a tool rather than a rule. If I write a haiku describing a waterfall in a lush green forest, I'll make it a spring haiku. That same waterfall in a forest of fallen orange leaves will be an autumn haiku. A kigo like "waterfall" can help set the season of a haiku but does not necessarily define it in and of itself. I could use "waterfall" in a haiku about love, which might not be seasonal at all.

To simplify even further, I can categorize a haiku according to the season I'm in when I write it, even if a kigo used is designated for another season. If I observe an owl early in the year, I write a spring haiku. I write an autumn haiku if I hear that same owl hooting near Halloween. Never mind that "owl" is considered a winter kigo; that season would not accurately apply to the haiku expression of my lived experience.

If you're writing haiku, use kigo when appropriate, but don't regard assigning it to a specific season absolutely necessary. Write your experiences with creativity and authenticity without feeling like you have to adhere to stringent guidelines. And if you're reading haiku, you shouldn't have to identify kigo to determine the setting. An engaging haiku, as a whole, will express everything you need to experience without requiring an analysis of the poem's structural details. You'll know a good haiku when you write one or read one.

Kireji: Two Becomes One

Another key element within the concise structure of haiku is the *kireji*, or "cutting word." In English haiku, a kireji can be a word or punctuation such as an em dash, ellipsis or exclamation mark, or it could simply be a natural pause. Kireji act as the vital link between the two parts of a haiku: a present-tense image or observation juxtaposed with a separate image, perception or impression. It aids the reader in reconciling these elements to complete the poem's picture. Let's examine my completed haiku to illustrate this principle.

azure sky
among clouds
thoughts drift

The first part of this haiku, "azure sky," captures a present tense observation, followed by the second part, "among clouds thoughts drift." "Sky" and "clouds" are the images that are juxtaposed with "thoughts." Reading this haiku in one breath, you should be able to detect the natural pause after "sky" before the second half, giving you a complete picture of the poem. You can also write it this way:

azure sky—
among clouds
thoughts drift

The em dash clarifies the shift while adding a nuance of suddenness and separation. In the case of this specific haiku, I prefer not to include the em dash as a kireji. I feel the natural pause after "sky" is sufficient enough on its own; however, such a choice is up to each author to decide.

Completing the Picture

Haiku are built from various components, but their success derives from the synergy of these parts and how they complement each other. A well-crafted haiku should evoke a strong impression, showcasing the poet's skill in weaving its elements together. Let's delve deeper into my "azure sky" haiku to explore my thought process when writing it.

"Azure sky" sets the scene with a daytime atmosphere and pleasant weather, where one might find clouds drifting by. If you have ever looked up and seen clouds in the sky on a nice day, perhaps you started to notice other things around you, like a warm breeze, the sound of rustling leaves or birds singing, or maybe catching the scent of flowers in the air. It may remind you of a lovely picnic long ago when the sky looked similar. Perhaps you're thinking of fond memories of that picnic, maybe with someone who makes you smile, or someone no longer present, bringing a touch of melancholy to your thoughts.

Or maybe you recall a time when you were in a hospital, gazing through a window at a blue sky, wishing you were outside to experience it fully. Or the beauty of the sky when you attended a funeral and how your thoughts inevitably drifted away.

If asked, "How does the sky equate to thoughts?" you might not have a clue what the answer to such a silly sounding question might be. However, suppose the six brief words of my haiku managed to reach inside to stir emotions and awaken memories. In that case, you, my friend, have made the connection and experienced the essence of haiku.

Grammar and Punctuation

In the spirit of brevity and capturing the flow of a moment in time with simplicity, haiku are typically written without capitalization and punctuation. It is often a matter of preference for poets to choose if and when they capitalize words or add punctuation to their haiku. For instance, I always capitalize some words, such as the word "I," proper names and holidays. They don't look or feel right to me otherwise.

Punctuation can be trickier. Some haiku poets disdain punctuation of any kind, feeling that if a phrase needs punctuation to illustrate a break or prevent the haiku from sounding like a run-on sentence, it should be rewritten not to require it.

I agree; however, there are instances where I feel if adding an em dash or ellipsis enhances the feel of a haiku, I will use it, and I find exclamation marks and question marks are often necessary for specific usages. I always address these on a case-by-case basis.

As a general practice, one should become familiar with reading and composing haiku in lowercase and without punctuation since this minimalist approach aligns with the form's innate simplicity and immediacy.

The Evolution Begins

I've just scratched the surface of haiku's form, aiming to provide casual readers with a solid foundation for understanding its structure and objectives. If you expand your study, you'll find many different styles and interpretations of haiku. For this book, though, I have provided the information necessary to turn through these pages to better understand what you're reading and extract the most from these poems.

I recommend readers give each haiku time to reflect on and contemplate any meaning received from it before moving on to the next one.

The Haiku Section includes five chapters: Spring, Summer, Autumn, Winter and Modern. In keeping with this book's "Evolution" theme, each chapter progresses from more accessible, conventional-style poems toward haiku that emphasize conciseness and juxtaposed imagery. I have written them with my preference for minimal capitalization and punctuation.

Thank you for reading, and please enjoy.

SPRING
HAIKU

spring incarnate
on the mirror lake
pink moon risen

studying life
the wren teaches
simplicity

jazz music
sung by the busker
chorus of warblers

heron wings push winds
from winter's grip
warm spring breeze

fledgling nest
high in the sky—
flight cancellation

two jays
one branch
spring skirmish

winter beats
a hasty retreat
lone woodpecker

heaven-scented
celestial beauty
pink andromeda

tantara pomp
stunning with grandeur
trumpet tree

turning tides—
imagining the moon
had oceans

blue kite
in clear skies
lost in thought

pull the string!
our kite tangled
in a rainbow

watching the world
behold its beauty
dark eyes fuchsia

winter thaw
the tip of my nose
warmed by jasmine

valley fog
morning birdsong
colors the gray

fresh bouquet
asking the wallflower
to dance

one tap—
the woodpecker
tries his luck

caught on the tip
of gravity's fang
blood moon waning

sweet hellos
on the telephone line
turtle doves

garden bluebells
the gray within
deepens

mockingbird
last night's dream
I can't recall

under a spell
before you know it
wild jasmine

whirring wings
sound of the unseen
hummingbird

ripples on the lake
underneath
a storm rises

breezy day
the butterfly glides
undaunted

somber gray
soothes wanderlust
the solace of rain

her fragrance
mingled with primrose
midnight rendezvous

first light—
through a dreamscape
footsteps in fog

where seeds sown
failed to flourish
a daisy prospers

too much blue
on the palette
a falling sky

the robin hops on
fresh mown lawn
we trade glances

roaring waterfall
learning you never said
I love you

sunlit daffodils
by the merry-go-round
the sandbox frozen

sorrow for
withered daffodils
if not for tulips

hardy hostas
replacing the dead
hardy hostas

roadside crocus
in the rear view
with winter[1]

idling through forests
past a calm lake
reflections appear[2]

fallen owl
feeling the weight
of silent trees[3]

blushing
in moonlight
cherry blossoms[4]

reaching
for the sky
star jasmine[5]

Endnotes

1. First published in *Folk Ku Journal Issue #3*—May 2024.
2. First published in *Heterodox Haiku Journal: Cutting Letters*—May 2024.
3. First published in the *Akitsu Quarterly Fall/Winter 2024 Issue*.
4. First published in *The Cicada's Cry Summer 2024 Issue*.
5. First published in *Tsuri Doro September/October 2024 Issue*.

SUMMER
HAIKU

gossamer moss
sways on cypress trees
southern charm breeze

praying mantis
meeting my gaze
zen garden moment

rains tarnish
church bell elegies
scent of white lily

storm clouds
rush the dusty savanna
winds sigh in relief

castle by the sea
marram grass dunes
echo ocean waves

wildflower scents
simply indescribable
I showed you instead

flamboyant flamingos
crowd the lagoon
showboat flotilla

caribbean breeze
swaying palmettos
dance the calypso

urban concrete
steaming the air
jazz cools the night

trade winds glide
through lush palms
the sun rages

pastel sky
showers wildflower fields
cosmos storm

in calm gloaming
curious fireflies
mimic stars

sunset fades...
an ocean of moonlight
ripples white dunes

footprints in sand
washed by infinite waves
lost legacies

fleeting thought
a shadow cast
by the dragonfly

whisper breeze
fluttering leaves
hummingbird wings

tiger lily
by the pond
twice the beauty

serendipity
what the butterfly
teaches

appearing
like clockwork
mirabilis bloom

no escape
for falling rain
calla lilies

orange zest
the sting of
paper cuts

red rose blooming
in the clouded mirror
black narcissus

raindrop ripples
a tsunami of
possibilities

sultry solstice
the jessamine wind
intoxicates

more than a match
for adamantine stone
rambling rose

where a snowman stood
the butterfly
flutters

king of the jungle
a brindle cat prowls
the garden

undiscovered
hummingbird feeder
paradise lost

bleached bones
the buzzard dreams of
could-have-beens

through dense canopy
the birch welcomes
sunrise

skyrockets
frozen in flight
crepe myrtle blooms

out from shade trees
two robins relish
the sprinkler

keeping calm
in rush hour traffic
wild chicory

summer romance
the rose moon
keeping secrets

terrarium fern
never knowing
a summer breeze

chess in the park
the magpie weighs
his next move

not sinking
not swimming
lotus blossom[1]

home from the islands
dad's Hawaiian shirt
on the memory bear[2]

still feeling good vibes
the beggar's
aloha shirt[3]

haymakers
landed in the yard
knock out roses[4]

Endnotes

1. First published in *The Heron's Nest*—June 2024.
2. First published in *The Asahi Shimbun*—June 21, 2024.
3. First published in *The Asahi Shimbun*—October 18, 2024.
4. First published in *Heterodox Haiku Journal: Cutting Letters*—May 2024 and nominated for a 2025 *Best of the Net Poetry Award.*

AUTUMN
HAIKU

pearls strung across
rainbow heavens
milky way sunset

cinnamon-scented
pumpkin spice latte
autumn in the air

sawmill sounds
swept on the wind
oaks tremble

leaps of faith
against all odds
salmon run

fallen leaves
caught in winter's grip
morning frost

street lamps
showing the moon
what it's missing

early stage
golden opportunity
ginkgo sapling

knowing the way
but not showing the way
fallen leaves

lip balm
making frightful winds
more kissable

autumn galaxy of
orange and red stars
sweetgum tree

taffy apples
irresistible
for just one month

grumpy neighbor
raking leaves
not a tree in his yard

abandoned barn
still feels like
work to do

cornucopia
a holiday abundance
of family strife

lone butterfly
sailing fickle winds
of melancholy

little black dress
proper for any
eclipse

fallen leaves
revelations of
unseen nests

autumn wind
shaping memories of
summer breezes

apple festival
bushels full of
Americana

under the fig tree
golden leaves
enlighten

sugar rush
the last coneflower found by
the honey bee

caught between

chaos and creation

dragon's claw

whirling turmoil

blots the stillness of night

bats in the belfry

black cat

dressed to

the nines

night owl
proving you're not alone
in the dark

happy children
carving pumpkins
toothless smiles abound

secret truce
once the farmer leaves
scarecrow and crow

days without you
all the asters
I never beheld

tree to tree
the spider builds
a nation

lichen on oak
the old tree
feeling older

building to
a fever pitch
touch-me-nots

getting our
stories straight
hedgerow

at one with nature
like no other
stick bug

sinking into
the comfort zone
amber sunset

cloudless sulphur
crossing the path
a change in the wind

distant owl call
one faint reply
in quiet fog

fording the river
of ochre silt
my feet of clay

frost glitters
in komorebi
the sleepy willow

an animal's cry
the darkness of night
turns blacker[1]

roaring fireplace
the dog pulls her bed
closer[2]

Endnotes

1. First published in *Kokako Issue* #41—September 2024
2. First published in the *Akitsu Quarterly Fall/Winter* 2024 *Issue.*

WINTER
HAIKU

lamplight snow
glows in twilight mystique
shivers melt

fallen leaves
beneath icy branches
holly berries shine

what tiny feet crept
through mist and snow
only the trees know

trampling through snow
in a strange neighborhood
the snowman waves

balsam wreath
sprucing the country cottage
Christmas cheer within

silence follows snow
coating city boulevards
keeping the peace

snowflakes caught
on children's tongues
lost in the moment

frankincense and myrrh
memories of Christmas past
in scented smoke

by the riverwalk
a snowman returns
my smile

two heart ornaments
on the Christmas tree
each for you and me

sprig of mistletoe
pinned on the old maid's door
all the berries gone

chimney smoke escapes
the snowbound cabin
welcome signals

dressed for winter
in early spring sun
unzipped parka

burning cold hands
throwing snowballs
back to childhood

shave cream
on gray whiskers
winter approaches

lighthouse burning bright
clad in wind whipped ice
forces of nature

town square Christmas tree
carolers join hand in hand
joy sung to the world

mustang in snow
charging through dreams
of reindeer flight

cookies and milk
left out for Santa
dad's favorite too!

Santa on the way
the struggle to
fall asleep

winter solstice
my longest day
without you

breath fog
secrets revealed in
icy moonlight

snow angels
hands together
melting hearts

lost in tatters
of crumpled paper
unwrapped gifts

winter
on the horizon
flock of starlings

every trick
in the book
red fox

icy gulag
infinite tears
wept in dust

deep in snowy pines
breathing evergreen
deep within

hastening my pace
the snowman's eyes
twinkle

after the vulture
a feathered angel
left in snow

ground blizzard
traffic lights turn red
for no one

shoveled parking space
standing room only
indoors

cold moon
crossing names off
the Christmas list

cranky neighbor
the snowball
on target

arctic blast
the dog finally willing
to try his booties

whisper snowfall
hickory crackles
on the hearth

frosted windows
clearly visible
memory loss[1]

creeping fog
only the lighthouse
knows[2]

elf on a shelf
the secrets
he must know[3]

yuletide spirit
the icicle
melting[4]

Endnotes

1. First published in *Five Fleas Itchy Poetry*—April 22, 2024.
2. First published in the *Akitsu Quarterly Fall/Winter* 2024 *Issue*.
3. First published in the Haiku Society of America's *Members Anthology* 2024.
4. First published in the *Wales Haiku Journal Winter* 24/25 *Issue*.

MODERN
HAIKU

steam train chanting
smokestack rhythms
mantra in motion

missed in the hustle
of morning routine
child's scribbled poem

green eyes
the color between
moonlight and dreams

cigarette ash
tapped on linoleum
still no news

our parting point—
promising we'd never
say goodbye

no words accompany
your tears...
I shiver

harmonizing life
between lullabies
and elegies

chasing stars...
sunlight returns
awakening dreams

roads traveled
through ancient lands
grandpa's stories

street musician
playing magic for a crowd
of one

birth certificate
faded and frayed
feeling my age

bringing dinner home
hoping for one good
fortune cookie

grasping straws
for one last try at love—
a raven takes flight

late night cinema
replaying cherished scenes
from memory

waking moon
illuminating dreams
and nightmares unseen

knock at the door—
wondering why the doorbell
wasn't used

three spins
no clue what the dog
is looking for

turning my pillow
to the cool side
her apology

ray of sunshine
in a frosty world
lemon cupcake

chopped onions
remembering
mom's kitchen

senior at the gym
adding weight
to longevity

neighbor's loud music
still softer than
their disharmony

decaying orbit
the gravity of
our relationship

greed of nations
lions convene
to zebra's dismay

gold embossed coin
impressions of
high value

gum drops
refusing to
go green

counted sheep
flooding the meadow
of insomnia

five o'clock shadow
meeting the therapist
after work

head lice
another excuse to
not like the new kid

candelabra
shadows still flicker
with you gone

magnetic storm
the lightning strike of
eye contact

lucky stars
the precious secrets
they've been told

at every core
layers of soul searching
peeled away

nostalgia
on crushed ice
shaken, not stirred

under the breaking
of eternal vows
diamond dust

each sip
rich with reflection
pennyroyal tea

queen's gambit
not the pawn's
strategy

cloud nine
eight tragedies
below

watching smoke
twist in mirrors
missing tricks

space by the old man
on the park bench
always space

surgical cuts
with cold precision
toxic romance

down a blind alley
feeling our way
through the dark

shadows creep
past the clock tower
another bell tolls

in the pall of dawn
light from the neighbor's attic
untold secrets seen

recurring nightmare
the sense of belonging
in another dream

in the hum
of routine traffic
a siren song

heavenly body
drawn to the gravity
of your orbit

silk spun words
tangled in a web of
feminine charm

coming in
for a smooth landing
blown kisses

morning hug
even in daylight
stars align

turning pages
a love story
continues

surprise birthday cake
another year
cancer-free

one
not the other
double entendre

facing the day—
which skin will I
choose today?

visiting papa
a stop outside to
feed his pigeons

plexiglas chairs on
polyurethane floors
footprints on the moon

timbre of sitars
in black light panorama
psychedelia

ambling through town
finding friendly strangers
not on the map

spiral staircase
the vertigo of
twisted truths[1]

tornado warning
that look in
your eyes[2]

Endnotes

1. First published in *Five Fleas Itchy Poetry*—April 22, 2024.
2. First published in *Haiku In Action*—May 3, 2024.

SECTION II
SENRYU

*"Poetry is when an emotion has found its thought
and the thought has found words."*

—Robert Frost

Now that you're familiar with haiku, you're well on your way to understanding senryu. Both follow the same form, structure and guidelines for capitalization and punctuation. The main difference is that while haiku often focus on nature, senyru delve into *human* nature.

Senryu can be humorous, ironic, cynical, or even horrifying, with subject matter ranging from whimsical and amusing to dark and disturbing. And just like with haiku, the traditional 5-7-5 syllable count rule in senryu can be ignored for creative expression and succinctness.

In the following senryu, I invite you to discover moments of laughter and thought-provoking insights.

driving too fast
spinning on black ice
crash course in karma

suggesting dutch treat
after the first date
also the last date

lucky rabbit foot
bad luck for the bunny
no luck for me

retirement home
cover band
golden oldies

surreal moment—
finding the last cookie
left for me

plastic-covered
living room
never lived in

guided tour
of the lighthouse
literally

too cool
for umbrellas
soggy teens

Spring chill
neighbors eyeing
Christmas lights

trigger warning—
family reunion
invitation

holiday banquet
a time to give thanks
for sweatpants

Sunday pub crawl
seven long days
to confession

earthquake tremor
the congregation
prays harder

nonpartisan to
ideologic stigmas
dogs chase the mailman

hot sauce in my eye
trying not to wink
at the waiter

gingham print
diary cover
checkered past

she loves her she shed
thankfully leaving him
alone in the he house

cold front moving in
forecast for missed
anniversary

streaking with
pen and paper
flash fiction

scarlet letters
dished in tabloid news
alphabet soup

reaching into my bag
of tricks...
a poem!

life's oddities
pondering awfully good
oxymorons

coat check girl
crossing the rubicon of
hat check girl

rat trap tripped—
instant regret over
snap decisions

secret recipe
an added dash of
wish I could say

borrowed socks
following strangely
in your footsteps

em dash—
where words lead
it follows

colorful
black and white
classic John Wayne

vitamin K
no other letters
worked either

house on magpie lane
we tell the realtor
to keep looking

opposites attract
white upholstery
and red wine

inspired décor
the bathroom's
outhouse theme

sterling tea set
for special occasions
your paper cup

mass destruction!
yet oddly rooting for
Godzilla

never quite sure
which way the wind will blow
parachute toy[1]

wardrobe attire
wondering which suit
I'll be buried in[2]

debate team
moment of silence
elevator ride[3]

early sign
of coming rain
forgotten umbrella[4]

lemon juice
with a twist of irony—
jumbo shrimp[5]

the Lord giveth

and the Lord taketh away

church bingo[6]

Endnotes

1. First published in *The Asahi Shimbun*—November 1, 2024.
2. First published in *Horror Senryu Journal*—June 25, 2024.
3. First published in *Failed Haiku Issue #100*—June 2024.
4. First published in *Failed Haiku Issue #100*—June 2024.
5. First published in *Failed Haiku Issue #100*—June 2024.
6. First published in *Failed Haiku Issue #100*—June 2024.

SECTION III
TANKA

If you are aware of the common three-line, 5-7-5 syllable pattern description of traditional haiku, perhaps you're also familiar with tanka and its traditional five-line composition framed around a 5-7-5-7-7 syllable pattern. As with haiku, the unique structure of tanka has also undergone an evolution over time, adding to its allure.

Origin of Tanka

While haiku dates back about 300 years, tanka traces its origins nearly 1,200 years ago to Japan's 9th-century Heian Period. When people of the era were courting, on the day after a date, the man would compose a tanka and send it to the woman as a "love letter" of sorts, writing of his thoughts on their time spent together. He, in turn, could expect a reply in kind—that is, if all went well on their date.

The traditional purpose of the tanka is to express emotions and personal reflection. Its style has undergone many changes over the centuries, perhaps the most significant of which occurred some 1,000 years into its run.

Evolution of Tanka

In the late 19th century, a Japanese poet named Tekkan Yosano (1873-1935) became frustrated with the style of tanka poets were writing. He felt that poets of the era were not only restricted by conforming to tanka's traditional 31-syllable pattern but the poetry being produced merely imitated works of the past millennium, leaving them unimaginative and uninspiring. Yosano drew attention to his beliefs by saying so in a boldly stated article he wrote for a prominent Japanese newspaper in 1894 advocating for the reform of tanka poetry.

Other acclaimed poets joined Yosano in his quest, perhaps most notably the great haiku and tanka poet Masaoka Shiki (1867-1902). Shiki also brought with him the concept of *shasei* to tanka. *Shasei*, or "sketch from life," is a style in which the poet writes what he sees to directly transmit his experience to the reader. To me, *shasei* in tanka is similar to capturing a "fleeting moment" with haiku.

The time was ripe for change to take hold as Japan's traditional feudal system began to disappear. In addition, Western influences started manifesting themselves in Japan's culture. Led by Yosano, Shiki and others, tanka reform was formally acknowledged and accepted in 1910.

Elements and Structure of Tanka

Tanka consists of two parts:

1. The upper three lines of the tanka (*kami no ku*) describe an image, scene, setting or experience.
2. The lower two lines of the tanka (*shimo no ku*) express the author's feelings or thoughts on the poem's first part, often comparing them using a tangible element, metaphor or analogy.

A turn or pivot connects the two parts, most often occurring in the third line, comprised of a word or expression that changes the tone or perception of the first half while also relating to the second half of the tanka, bringing synergy to the poem. This "turn" is a crucial element of tanka, as it often introduces a new perspective or layer of meaning, enhancing the poem's emotional impact. It's like a twist in a story that changes the reader's understanding or perspective of the narrative. In this way, tanka has a juxtaposition similar to that of haiku, that of something tangible paired with a reflection or emotion to complete the poem.

When combining these elements, a well-crafted tanka should flow as one sentence or thought. The reader should be able to visualize the subject, get a sense of the turn, and then interpret the reflection as to how it connects to the subject in one smooth sequence with deep meaning or intention. You will get a feel for this as you read my tanka through this book section.

The first two poems in this section follow traditional tanka characteristics. From there, I break form, evolving away from restrictive syllable counts into various freeform subject matter with entertaining examples of juxtapositional and *shasei* tanka.

Please enjoy!

tomorrows echo
our remembrances today
keepsakes of us
hand in hand on our journey
we embrace the infinite

coda of nightfall
torn away from lyric dreams
of my sweet soubrette
under stars we'll meet again
and dance to moonlight music

your wounded heart
bleeds in
poetic prose
mine a bandage
thirsty for words

words on pages
verse after verse
spinning a story
told from the heart
heard by a heart

your radiant rose
bloomed bright
in the mirror
turning revealed
petals in dust

led by the light
of heavenly stars
on earth
glorious guiding
luminaria

an iota of light
exiles darkness
the trees
the rain
and I remain

dawn chorus
fractures
nightly calm
darkness ebbs
in birdsong

sea foam
sprays silken stone
at sundown
forgiven tides
quietly disappear

curious
to peek behind
the curtain
finding myself
already there

sweet tea
on the veranda
under haint blue
not a spirit
among us[1]

sparks struck
at kindling
late into night
cold and drowsy
the fire waits

the day's release
bares secrets
in cool darkness
long before dawn
our night smolders

downwind
of a lilac tree
perfume colors
an azure breeze
where lovers breathe

chase the wind
to wildwood trees
where autumn breathes
each leaf brushing your cheek
a tender kiss from me

by the window
where I watched you leave
the curtain flaps
in a gentle breeze
and nothing more

promise of rain
striping the window
where she dwells
on promises
not hers to keep

when the path
we walk together
reaches an end
who will look to see
where we've gone?

until we meet again
dusk awakens night
with anxious hands
I push the stars
into tomorrow

autumn breeze
through sparse maples
awakening silence
of songbirds
taken flight

watching you sleep
peacefully serene
in moonstruck light
I fade from this world
awake in your dream

faraway star
sanguine in
the radiant night
a fire inside
destined to burn

while dragonflies
water dance
the gentle river
carries them
together

our wedding album
seeing you today
just as I did then
knowing we'll forever
grow young together

finding father's
prayer card under
mother's—
has it really been
that long ago?

a drifter
plays his harmonica
on the train
rolling into Memphis
my toe taps

in-flight
entertainment
the moving pictures
I watch through
the window

poke and probe
the abyss
of your silence
still no sign
of us[2]

so full of empty
only space remains
for echoes...
whisper your voice
deafen my darkness[3]

two coins
head over tails
in the wishing well
across time and space
the secrets they share[4]

Endnotes

1. Haint blue is a pale shade of blue-green commonly used to paint porch ceilings and doors of homes in the Southeastern United States to keep haints, or ghosts, from entering the home. The tradition originates from early 19th century Gullah culture.
2. First published in *Folk Ku Journal Issue #3*—May 2024.
3. First published in The Tanka Society of America's *Ribbons Fall/Winter 2024, Volume 20, Number 2 Edition.*
4. First published in The Tanka Society of America's *Laurels Issue #3*—February 2025.

SECTION IV
HAIBUN

Welcome to the final section of this book, poised to explore haibun, a form of poetry that I've grown quite fond of.

Haibun originated in 17th-century Japan from legendary poet Matsuo Basho; however, the first English-language haibun appeared in the early 1960s, making it a comparatively new short-form writing style.

Put simply, haibun is a blend of prose and haiku poetry. Each element relies on its strengths to work together while remaining independent, simultaneously contrasting and complementing each other. The distinctive mix of these elements combine to weave a rich tapestry of writing to create a powerful haibun.

While haibun does have some common guidelines and suggestions directing its form, it also offers a wide range of creative freedom, allowing for individual interpretation and expression. This introduction aims to equip you with enough knowledge to appreciate and enjoy the haibun I've published in this book.

Prose: Show Me, Don't Tell Me

Haibun prose often describes a scene, character, event or memorable moment but can be about anything, whether fact-based or fictitious. The prose of haibun is usually written in the present tense to provide a sense of "being there" for the reader, but it can also be a second, or third-person narrative.

A haibun's prose should employ powerful, descriptive, evocative and concise writing colored with vivid imagery. It should draw readers in, compelling them to learn more about its story. Writers should include only necessary wording without redundancy.

Most importantly, the prose should only show, not tell, leaving the reader to interpret the haibun uniquely and draw conclusions about its meaning.

Haiku: Fuel for the Fire

Haiku are integral in creating well-written haibun. Without good haiku, no amount of brilliant prose will allow for haibun to succeed. For this reason, haiku are generally created first before setting out to write prose for haibun.

Haiku adds to or enhances the meaning of the prose, offering a reflection or complementary quality to the subject or theme and often including a sharp juxtaposed quality. As in the case of prose, haiku adopts a "show, don't tell" approach, leaving the reader to his own interpretation. In this way, creating effective interaction between the prose and haiku leads to the sum of both becoming a greater, more compelling haibun.

The Title: Use It, Don't Lose It

Unlike haiku and tanka, haibun include titles. A title provides the writer with another component to add a compelling descriptive element to the haibun that can interact with the prose and haiku to augment the reader's impression of the haibun. Again, the title should show, not tell, and be as innovative as the prose and haiku. If you're writing a haibun about red roses, the last thing you want for a title is "Red Roses." Haibun should always take advantage of the creative opportunity for enhancement by utilizing an intriguing or imaginative title.

A Final Word on Haibun

I enjoy combining my passion for haiku and creative writing to compose haibun. I like to think of the prose as drawing readers into the story, painting a picture that leads you curiously further and further in before the haiku strikes like a lightning bolt.

When I write a haibun, I always have an idea of what I'm writing about, but if crafted correctly, that idea will always be a mystery to everyone else. There is always more than one way to interpret my haibun, and in some cases, many ways to interpret them.

And that is the beauty of haibun—they exist to entertain, provoke thought and reveal meaning according to each reader in their own way.

Smokestack Lightning

slow dance
gilded eyes glitter
in neon lights

Deceptive in its naive simplicity, a first kiss can be an ever-lasting force of nature if you're very lucky. A firestorm of seconds or minutes capable of raging through a lifetime. Often, you sense it coming, but sometimes it leaps panther-like, spontaneous and ferocious. Evolution ignites animal instinct. Lips touch, locking sublimely in a synchronous rhythm. Mouths dance a velvet tango. Shivers tingle. Hands glide as bodies yearn to meld. Senses surrender, wildly overwhelmed, tangled in perfumed passion. A soft moan proves you're not alone in your reverie, and all seems well in the universe far, far away on your ninth cloud, where time blurs and space melts into the ether.

When at last you see each other's eyes and reclaim breath so sweetly stolen, everything has irrevocably changed. Maybe friends, maybe strangers, but never the same. Every glance stirs a reminder. Every thought a seduction. Every butterfly a keepsake. A flame forever searing the molten skin of your soul.

misty moonlight
a car horn screams
for the parking space

Amitié Amoureuse

Tommy the bartender had a real knack for solving Jake's problems. Four bourbons deep, Jake spilled his guts. Tommy listened, then told Jake that, on the one hand, she would never trust him. On the other hand, he could never trust her. There was a third hand, but Tommy took a mai tai to the busty blonde down the bar and mumbled something Jake didn't catch. He wasn't sure Tommy solved the problem, but the fifth bourbon appeared, and that was just fine. Good old Tommy.

another time
another place
forget-me-nots

Afterparty

Bob loved his wife, but her bizarre fascination with the occult got out of hand once she became obsessed with the spirit world. Enough was enough. Bob corralled all his skeptic friends and decided to host an intervention party complete with a medium. What a kook! She spread a black velvet cover over their dining table, complete with tarot cards, candles and a crystal ball perched on a pewter clawed hand of some sort. She had the whole schtick going on. Candles were lit, lights went out, and they all sat around the table, joining hands. Time to get this nonsense over with, once and for all.

at the séance
a telephone ring
no one will answer

Panorama

She died in her sleep, leaving him to find her this morning by his side. Young and unmarried, sharing a loving life together. In his grief, he must have reverted to their morning routine before I arrived. Coffee is brewing, and the TV is on and tuned to a game show.

tears for the fallen
Jan from Burbank passes on
showcase number one

His answers follow my questions, peppered with "I can't believe it" and "What do I do now?" as he struggles to comprehend his new reality. I genuinely feel bad for him and offer my sincere condolences with earnest concern.

care for the stricken
Mitzi leaves dog hair
on my pants

The body snatchers arrive and go upstairs. "What happens now?" Well, I know it isn't going to be glamorous or anything he will want to see and remember for the rest of his life. Out of compassion, I am determined to do my best to help the poor guy avoid that.

grace for the living
my latte cooling
in the car

I succeed at distracting him when I hear feet tramping down the stairs. One of the snatchers missteps at the bottom, uttering a "dammit!" while bouncing the corpse's head off a wall.

And there he goes, my efforts undone, turning around to see his sweetheart zipped up in a body bag unceremoniously hauled off head first out the front door and into the back of a drab white municipal van.

Numb disbelief.

"And that's it," he mutters. "One day, you're laughing and loving your soulmate, and the next, they're wrapped in plastic and carried out like garbage. Done. That's it."

I can't argue with him. He pretty much has the whole tragic picture, as he sees it anyway.

> *prayer for the dead*
> *still time to meet the boys*
> *for breakfast*

Hive Mind

Often, I see people around me as ants. Gray. I endeavor to make a conscious effort to remember they are humans. Roaming about from place to place, going nowhere. Have none of them read Thoreau?! Green. Annoying chirrup squeaks of their insect-like language. They crawl on my skin. Yellow. Creep under my skin. Orange. I'm beginning to think I'm the only human, yet the ants give me no regard. Red. Am I something more? Perhaps if I were a god. But if I'm the only human among these ants, would I not be a god?

They *are* ants. I *am* a god.

vantablack[1]
could we be more
in the dark?

Left Turn at Albuquerque

The roadrunner used to actually blow up the coyote. I learned about dynamite that way. You could either wire it to a box with a plunger you pushed from a distance, or you could light a fuse with a match and throw it. Years later, those scenes were cut from cartoons to make sure kids didn't try anything like that at home. Scenes with guns, anvils and sledgehammers too. All edited out. I never saw any characters push a stranger in front of an oncoming train though. I wonder which cartoon showed that.

seeking directions
I walk in the shadow
of a cloud

Chromatic Sense

If Debussy painted music, his notes might cascade forth in a lustrous cerulean hue, pooling in a velvety smooth and soothing lake. With each graceful rendering, one could float on timeless waves, again and again, aglow in sonic iridescence. Adrift...the lake would soon become a vast, serene ocean.

clair de lune
not all beauty
is fleeting

Indigo Flame[2]

Yesterday was unusually cool, but the heat wave has resumed. Through the wrought iron fence, a duskywing flutters past a rose whose pink petals briefly waver. Tracing dizzying zigzags across the yard, it suddenly comes to rest on the back of my hand. We study each other here in the calm shade, then a gentle flicker of wings, and I'm left alone again. How quickly yesterday's breeze is forgotten.

windswept day
in and out of my thoughts
a butterfly

It Was the Owl That Shrieked[3]

She could barely see beyond the crust of corrosion distorting her peripheral vision. Lost in thought, she always said there were nuances between tarnish and patina, and hardly worth discussing. She could shine whenever she chose to.

setting the tone
drawing every line
crossing her path

Someone will polish her silver soul, a warrior with well-oiled armor in summer glory. No rust would mar the skin. A sun bears down on her parasol as she watches the horizon, and then another autumn arrives, bringing dust in its amber wake.

one cloud
scent of petrichor
in the clarion sky

The irony of oxidation is that it protects what it hides. Rainbow hues mask her frayed edges. There's simply too much oxygen. No fault of her own.

With her black spade, she digs a hole by the path that waits for the coming Spring, giving no thought to who might toss dirt on her heirloom grave.

Macbeth in her words
Shakespeare is a hard act
to follow

Juice Just as Sweet[4]

From my earliest memories, I rarely knew my mother to be anywhere except by the television watching soap operas, Merv Griffin, and Walter Cronkite. It was a habit I picked up from her, though I've been learning new things lately. Since she had them take the TV out of her room, I always find her waiting for me in the garden area wearing the most charming smile. I wheel her casually around as she marvels at everything from the changing maples to fresh air and fragrant breezes. I never knew that was the alyssum I smelled until she mentioned it one afternoon. God willing, I hope to take her to see the holiday decorations tomorrow. There's a chance of rain, and she already has her umbrella waiting.

sunset lingers...
once more
around the park

Endnotes

1. Vantablack is a super-black coating created by Ben Jensen of Surrey NanoSystems in 2014. It is able to absorb up to 99.965% of visible light, laying claim to being the world's darkest known pigment.
2. "Indigo Flame" was first published in *Cattails Spring/ April 2025 Issue.*
3. "It Was the Owl That Shrieked" was first published in *The Pan Haiku Review Haibun & Tanka-bun Edition— Winter 2024.*
4. "Juice Just as Sweet" was first published in *The Pan Haiku Review Haibun & Tanka-bun Edition—Winter* 2024.

Acknowledgements

My wife, Hollie, is not just a loyal companion to my writing process, but also a significant contributor to this book. Her willingness to help with proofing and editing, her unwavering support and her influence on my personal growth have all made this book what it is. She makes me a better person, and in turn, this book a better book.

Submitting my work to publications is an enjoyable way for me to connect with my fellow poets. I want to express my sincere thanks to all the publishers and editors who saw value in my work and included it in their publications. It is a great honor to be counted among my peers.

I am particularly grateful to all the editors who graciously take the time to offer their expertise in the form of helpful critiques and advice, with special mention this time around to Jerome Berglund, Sonam Chhoki, Terri French, Jeff Hoagland, David McMurray, Keith Polette, Alan Summers and Susan Weaver.

And finally, my deepest gratitude goes to you, the reader. Thank you for investing your valuable time in reading my book. I sincerely hope it proved to be an enjoyable and enriching experience for you. Your interest in my work is truly humbling.

If you enjoyed my poetry, please consider rating this book or submitting a review from where you purchased it.

Thank you!

About the Author

Leon Tefft is a writer, poet and author of *Haiku Evolution* and *Haiku Traditions*.

Born and raised in Chicago, Illinois, Leon's love of poetry originated with the first haiku he wrote as a teenager, spurring decades of creative writing expressed though poetry and short story fiction. His poetry has appeared in numerous online and print publications. He is a member of the Haiku Society of America and the Tanka Society of America.

Leon draws inspiration for his creativity from a wide range of unique experiences throughout his life. His resume includes writer, artist, actor, celebrity bodyguard, trader and business owner. He is an avid reader with noted interests in history, philosophy and photography.

Leon is a retired police officer with 30 years of distinguished service to his hometown City of Chicago. He currently resides in South Carolina with his wife, Hollie.